MUNICH, BAVARIA AND SALZBURG
for
TRAVELERS

-The total guide-

The comprehensive traveling guide for all your traveling needs.

© 2019 by THE TOTAL TRAVEL GUIDE COMPANY
© 2019 by BRENDA PUBLISHING

PUBLISHED BY

TABLE OF CONTENTS

Why do we claim our guides are "total guides"?

Why are they really comprehensive?

Because we do almost anything to make sure that all the main issues relevant to the conscious traveler are covered in our guides.

We hate the typical boring travel guides chocked up with standard information you can readily find on the Internet.

We travel, we research other guides, we talk to locals, we ask friends, we ask friends of friends,

we do whatever it takes to make sure that we have you covered. All the angles! This is how we get the best tips, the most valuable for every one of our travel destinations.

That is where we got the best tips, the most valuable ones about our travel destinations.

All our guides are reviewed and edited by a "local" writer to make sure that the guide is one of its kind, comprehensive, fun and interesting. We prefer not to add too many maps or photos since you can have all that on the internet. We prefer to focus the content on tips and unique data that makes worthwhile to buy our total guides.

We use different approaches for each city, as each destination is unique. You will be able to verify that our guides are not standardized. Each one is different because each place is different. And you will enjoy the difference,

Our production team is very proud of our guides. We hope you will enjoy the reading and take full advantage of your traveling.   !

Introduction

Neuschwanstein Castle – Photo credit: pixabay.com

If you are looking for a great place to spend your holiday, there is no better choice than the beautiful land of Bavaria, with its center star being represented by the elegant Munich. At a close distance, you can find the splendid Salzburg, completing your journey and creating memories that you are going to cherish for many years to come. This book is dedicated to all those who want to travel to this part of Europe, being structured into chapters for easy access to the desired information.

To help you plan the best traveling adventure, the book has been structured into three main sections: Munich, Bavaria and Salzburg. Each section has been further divided into chapters. The first chapter is dedicated to the reasons why you should consider visiting either of these three destinations. In the second chapter, you can find traveling advice provided by locals living in the above-mentioned areas. The third chapter is dedicated to budget traveling, while the fourth concentrates on the basic travel information that you might find useful.

In the fifth chapter, you can find details on the public transportation system and how you can use it for a comfortable traveling experience. The sixth chapter presents the finest hotels and restaurants in Munich, Bavaria and Salzburg. In the seventh chapter, readers can find information on the cultural agenda of each of the three destinations, while the last chapter in each section includes details about the best shopping opportunities. The book ends with a conclusion, summing up the information that was presented here.

If you want to have the best traveling experience, read this book before you actually go on the trip. The main purpose of this book is to make your traveling experience rewarding, helping you create memories that you are going to cherish for a long time to come.

Why Visit Munich?

Munich Olympia Tower – Photo credit: pixabay.com

Munich, the capital of Bavaria, is one of the most beautiful cities in the world, being visited by over 70 million people each year. As a tourist coming to this amazing German town, you cannot help but fall in love with its numerous attractions, elegant architecture and the wealth of events that are organized in different fields. There are sports events to be part of, exhibitions of art and the famous Oktoberfest, where you have the opportunity to taste the traditional German beers.

The city welcomes visitors from all around the world, having a very nice motto to entice them with: "Munich loves you" (Germ. München mag dich). As you will have the opportunity to discover, there are international flights that you can use to arrive here and an excellent public transportation system to use during your stay. In fact, due to the high quality of life, Munich was selected in 2013 as the world's most livable city. This may have something to do with the small town charm that Munich proudly possesses, despite being such a large urban area.

One of the main reasons you should consider visiting Munich is its royal Bavarian heritage. Everywhere you will turn, you will see the signs of this rich history, with its splendid architecture. Even the residents of Munich seem to have retained some of this elegance and you will definitely see that just by looking at how they dress and walk on the streets. During your time in Munich, you will want to sit at one of the outdoor cafes, steering your seat towards the street, in order to analyze the latest German fashion trends. If you come to this city in the summer, there are plenty of beer gardens to visit, offering you the possibility to try out different types of beer.

Munich is, without doubt, the lifestyle capital of Germany. There are plenty of opportunities for shopping, ranging from small boutiques to large shopping centers. Sports enthusiasts can enjoy the amazing football stadium of the famous Bayern Munich or visit the former Olympic village. The truth is that this modern and cosmopolitan city has something to offer to all those who come to it. It is the best place to enjoy the German lifestyle!

Munich Local Travel Advice

Oktoberfest - Photo credit: pixabay.com

If you have chosen Munich for your next destination, you should know that this is a relatively safe city. However, you might want to steer clear of the train station area at night and also avoid the Hasenbergel district. Also, be sure to watch your belongings in the U-Bahn (subway), as the muggers are quite agile and they can easily disappear with your camera equipment or other expensive items.

Germany might be the land of beer but you have to keep in mind that drinking alcohol in the pedestrianized areas of the historic center (Marienplatz included) is forbidden. You can drink as much as you want in pubs and beer gardens but avoid drinking alcohol right on the street, as you will get a fine. The police is quite strict on the alcohol consumption and this rule was given out, so as to keep the historic city center clear and peaceful. Keep in mind that the legal blood alcohol limit for drinking and driving is of 0.5 g/L. Do not drink excessively and then drive – this is especially valid around Oktoberfest, as the police often does random alcohol testing during this event.

Speaking about Oktoberfest, this will be the kind of event that you do not forget. We, locals, enjoy the event just as much as tourists. However, I must give you a piece of advice. Don't try to steal the beer mugs at Oktoberfest. There are policemen that check you when you leave the beer halls and it would be a shame to get a fine for a simple mug. There are souvenir shops where you can buy such a souvenir, so try to remain civil.

I can tell you that the parking is a problem in Munich, especially around the historic city center. The parking garages can be quite expensive, so you might consider a day ticket, as this is more advantage. Keep in mind that many of the parking spots are reserved for locals, so avoid parking your car in such a spot. Learn a little bit of German, a few essential phrases, as they will help you with such matters. Also, be prepared for the sudden weather changes and remember that smoking is forbidden in restaurants.

Munich on a Budget

Frauenkirche - Photo credit: pixabay.com

Despite of what everyone says about Germany, it is possible to travel to this country without spending a fortune. If you are under a tight budget, during your stay in Munich, you should consider using the public transportation system and choosing youth hostels for accommodation. Also, keep in mind that the most important sights of Munich are located in the historic city center, which means that they are also within walking distance.

From the main train station, it only takes a quarter of an hour in order to reach Marienplatz, one of the most beautiful squares of Munich. You can take a free city tour, these being offered by New Europe Tours (http://www.neweuropetours.eu/). Whether you decide to walk or take the bus tour, you can see the beautiful buildings of Munich, such as Frauenkirche (http://www.muenchner-dom.de/; +490892900820; Frauenplatz 12) or Hofbräuhaus (http://www.hofbraeuhaus.de/; +49089290136100; Platzl 9). I especially recommend the latter, as it is one of the most famous beer halls of Germany, having being built in 1598. You can also use the public transportation in order to visit Nymphenburg Palace (http://www.schloss-

13

nymphenburg.de/; +49089179080; Schloss Nymphenburg 1), which is located just half an hour from Munich.

If you want to save a lot of money on your travel, you should consider the City Tour Card. This is valid between 1 and 4 days, for the inner district or the entire network, providing free public transportation and discounts to over 70 tourist attractions, not only in Munich but also in the surrounding areas. The prices are different for the single and the group tickets; the card becomes valid the moment you use it to visit a tourist attraction or on the public transportation.

Among the attractions for which discounts are offered, there are: Segway Tours (http://www.munich.citysegwaytours.com; +4908923888798; Karlsplatz 4); Bier & Oktoberfest Museum (http://www.bier-und-oktoberfestmuseum.de/; +4908924231607; Sterneckerstrasse 2) and Allianz Arena (http://www.allianz-arena.de; +49089350948350: Werner-Heisenberg-Allee 25). The card also offers discounts to restaurants, cafes and beer halls, so do not hesitate to use it to its full potential. You can also use to satisfy your thirst for culture, seeing a play at the Deutsches Theater (http://www.deutsches-theater.de; +4908955234444; Schwanthaler Str.13) or at the Münchner Marionettentheater (http://muema-theater.de; +49089265712; Blumenstr. 32).

Munich Travel Basics

Munich Skyline - Photo credit: pixabay.com

The best time to visit Munich is at the end of September or at the beginning of October. You have guessed it right – this is the time when the famous Oktoberfest (http://www.oktoberfest.eu/) takes place. If you want to experience the true taste of Germany, there is no more suitable time and place than this amazing beer festival to do that.

In terms of weather, the best time to visit Munich is in the summer, between the months of June and August. The weather is warm (but not too warm) but you may need to carry an umbrella or better yet a rain coat, as the thunderstorms are quite frequent. In the winter, there are far less tourists, with the exception of the Christmas/New Year period. However, you must always remember that Munich is situated quite close to the Alps, so the weather is hard to predict, no matter the time of year.

You can arrive in Munich by plane; as it was already mentioned, there are both national and international flights that land on the Munich International Airport, which is located at 18 miles from the city center. From the airport, you can reach the city center, using the commuter train service. If you are coming from countries outside the European Union, you will need a valid passport; if you are planning on staying for more than 90 days in Munich, you will also need a visa. For those who are traveling from the countries of the European Union, the ID card is enough (no passport required).

Keep in mind that Munich is in the GMT+1 time zone (GMT+2 between April and October). Depending on the country from which you are traveling, you might experience jet lag and you will require one or two days to adapt. In Munich, there are standard European plugs for electricity, so you might need an adaptor plug in case you are coming from America. In terms or language, English is understood and spoken but it might be wise to learn a few German phrases. Also, remember that the currency of Germany is Euro, as in the rest of the countries that are part of the EU. If you need to change money, do it at the bank, so as to avoid paying a commission.

Public Transportation in Munich

U-Bahn Station Munich - Photo credit: pixabay.com

The public transportation system in Munich is excellent, consisting of the following choices: underground trains (U-Bahn), suburban trains (S-Bahn), trams and buses. You can easily recognize the subway stations, as these have a sign that has a white U on a background that is blue in color. The S-Bahn stations are easily recognizable as well, with the white S being depicted on a green background. As for the trams and the bus stops, these have a sign with a green H on a yellow background.

The good news is that the S-Bahn has stations throughout the entire city center of Munich. For example, you can leave from the main train station (Hauptbahnhof) and reach two of the most beautiful squares of Munich, meaning Marienplatz and

Karlsplatz. The S-Bahn also connects the other train station in Munich – East Station (Ostbahnhof) – with the same touristic attractions.

You do not need to purchase a different ticket every time you want to change the means of transportation, as the same ticket is valid for all. The tickets can be purchased from the blue vending machines that are found in the U-Bahn and S-Bahn stations. You can also purchase the tickets from the bus or tram stops, depending on the means of transportation you are interested in, or from the newspaper kiosks. The important thing to remember is that you validate the ticket before actually getting on the train; if you fail to do that, it is highly likely you will receive a fine (around 40 euro).

If you are interested in obtaining more information about the public transportation system in Munich, you can visit the information office from Marienplatz. Here, you can also obtain a free map with the different means of transportation and their routes. Also, you will receive valuable advice on the different types of tickets that can be purchased. There are three main categories to choose from, meaning single, stripe and day tickets. You can also benefit from free public transportation by purchasing the City Tour Card (remember that the transportation is free during the period for which the card is valid).

Best Hotels And Restaurants In Munich

Munich Hotel - Photo credit: pixabay.com

Munich has a wealth of beautiful hotels to choose from, each having something different to offer. From top luxury hotels to youth hostels, Munich caters to the tastes of even the most pretentious traveler. As for the restaurants, you have the opportunity to taste meals that belong to both the local and international cuisine.

Here are the best-choice hotels in Munich:

1. Hotel Lux

- Recently renovated
- Close to the Hofbräuhaus
- Modest furnished rooms
- Local art in each room

- Recommended – Ponyhof room (designed by Hans Langner)
- Great restaurant (with high prices however)
- Address: Ledererstr. 13
- Tel.: +4908945207300
- Website: http://www.munich.hotel-lux.info

2. Motel One

- European budget hotel
- Equipped with everything you may need (TV, air conditioning, Wi-Fi)
- Pay extra for breakfast
- You can eat sandwiches at the bar
- Great view over the Deutsches Museum
- Clever design
- Excellent service
- Address: Rablstr. 2
- Tel.: +4908944455580
- Website: http://www.motelone.com/

3. Euro Youth Hotel

Located right to the main train station

Recommended for those who are under a tight budget

Beautiful building (survived the second World War intact – it was once the luxurious Hotel Astoria)

Hostel with a tradition of over 17 years

Perfect blend between modern and traditional

Friendly service

Great bar

Address: Senefelderstr. 5

Tel.: +4908959908811

Website: http://www.euro-youth-hotel.de/

Here are the best restaurants in Munich:

1. Restaurant Mark's

- Perfect blend between French, Mediterranean and Asian cuisine

- Five-star service

- Renaissance charm

- Meals prepared from seasonal and fresh produce

- Menu changes daily

- Exceptional desserts

- Elegant music played at the piano

- Address: Neuturmstr. 1

- Tel.: +4908929098875

- Website: http://www.mandarinoriental.com/munich/dining/restaurant_marks/

2. Restaurant Davvero

- Mediterranean cuisine

- Perfect place for a romantic, candlelit dinner

- Beautiful interior, with high ceilings and elegant chandeliers

- Delicacies of Italian flavor

- Unique dining experience

- Best place to enjoy your meal – summer terrace

- Meals prepared by the famous chef, Giovanni Russo

- Address: Sophienstr. 28

- Tel.: +490895445551200

- Website: http://www.thecharleshotel.com/

3. Tegernseer Tal Bräuhaus

- Classic Bavarian cuisine

- Opportunity to taste traditional meals, such as the roast pork with dumpling or the cheese spread
- Great traditional music
- The waiters wear the German lederhosen
- Located right in the old part of the town
- Address: Tal 8
- Tel.: +49089222626
- Website: http://www.tegernseer-tal8.com/braeuhaus/

Cultural Opportunities In Munich

Munich Museum - Photo credit: pixabay.com

Munich is a cultural hub, with sumptuous palaces that house amazing art collections, theatres that present classic operas and unique attractions that you might never have thought of as culture. Start your cultural adventure with a visit to Munich Residenz (http://www.residenz-muenchen.de/; +49089290671; Residenzstr. 1). The formal royal palace has an amazing architecture and exquisite interior decorations, having over 130 apartments. Here, you can find the famous Cuvilliés Theatre – built in the Rococo style, in 1755, this theatre mounted the performance of the first opera that Mozart wrote.

If you enjoy classical music and opera, you need to visit Munich in the summer and take part in the Summer Opera Festival. This festival is organized within the National Theatre (http://www.staatsoper.de/; +49089218501; Max-Joseph-Platz 2), which is a located in a beautiful building as well, providing a feast for the eyes with its blend of gold, marble and crystal. Munich makes a positive impression on anyone who loves music, with its 61 theatres and 4 major orchestras. There is the amazing Munich Philharmonic Orchestra (http://www.mphil.de/), which a tradition dating from 1893, the Munich Chamber Orchestra and the prestigious Bavarian State Ballet.

As for art galleries, once you come to Munich, you have to check the three Pinakothek Art Galleries (http://www.pinakothek.de/). There are three different art galleries to visit, meaning Alte Pinakothek, Neue Pinakothek and Moderne Pinakothek. In the Old art gallery, you can find works belonging to renowned artists, such as Titian, Leonardo and Rubens. The New art gallery is dedicated to artists such as Goya, Monet and Cézanne. Modern art displays are present in the modern art gallery as well.

The Munich Glyptothek Museum (http://www.antike-am-koenigsplatz.mwn.de/; Königsplatz 3) is also interesting to visit, as this building has been after the neoclassical style and it houses amazing Greek antiquities, including the famous Temple of Aegina. Keep in mind that, for Germans, beer is culture too. Do not hesitate to visit the famous Hofbräuhaus, enjoying yourself to the maximum. After an entire day spent visiting, this might be the perfect way to end the day, relaxing and enjoying a traditional beer.

Shopping Opportunities In Munich

Munich Shopping - Photo credit: pixabay.com

The shopping experience in Munich is extraordinary to say the least. There are numerous opportunities for finding international labels, as well as designer fashion items. You can also shop for classic Bavarian products, such as Lederhosen and Dirndl. The shopping scene in Munich is beautiful and you should start your adventure with the Inner City. Here, you can find the Neuhauser und Kaufinger Strasse, a boulevard that is located between Marienplatz and Karlsplatz. A pedestrianized area, this is actually a busy shopping area, suitable for all budgets.

If you are interested in luxury shopping, it is recommended that you check out Theatinerstrasse, the street that connects Marienplatz with Odeonplatz. From there, you can visit the latest shopping center opened in Munich, Fünf Höfe. For international haute couture and luxury shopping, with world renowned brands, be sure to visit Maximilianstrasse as well. On the other hand, if you are searching for traditional souvenirs to offer to your loved ones, you should check out

Orlandostrasse. This street is located at a close distance from Hofbräuhaus; in fact, you can find a lovely souvenir shop inside this beer hall as well.

The trendiest shops in all of Munich can be found in the Gärtnerplatz Quartier, this being an area dedicated to the gay and lesbian scene. If you are looking for unique products to purchase, including in terms of clothing, these are the shops you should check out. As for bookworms, these should definitely consider visiting the Student Quarter. Located in the vicinity of the Munich University, it is the best place in Munich to find second-hand bookshops. Boutiques of artistic inspiration can be found on Schwabbing, a street that was frequented by artists in the 20th Century and still retains that special atmosphere today. For fresh fruits and vegetables, herbs and spices, do not hesitate to visit the Viktualienmarkt, the central food market of Munich. In winter, you can visit the traditional Christmas markets that are organized all over Munich, enjoying a cup of warm wine that has been spiced with rum for a unique taste.

Why Come To Bavaria?

Scheyern, Bavaria - Photo credit: pixabay.com

Bavaria is one of the most renowned regions of Germany, being chosen as a holiday destination by millions of tourists. Some arrive here, looking to discover the pristine nature, with the blue skies and the lakes that are crystal clear. There are beautiful places to discover all over Bavaria, including the famous Black Forest and the Alps that offer an exciting adventure any time of year. But nature is not the only thing that may persuade you to visit this part of Germany. There are over 100.000 architectural monuments to be discovered, many of them being located in or around small medieval towns.

Whether you will visit a small medieval town or a large, vibrant city such as Munich, you will definitely fall in love with the Bavarian traditions and enjoy the friendliness of locals. You will find plenty of opportunities for outdoor activities and recreation, no matter if you come in the summer or in the winter. In regard to culture, Bavaria has a wealth of attractions, including over 1200 museums. You can visit the places that have been listed as part of the UNESCO World Heritage sites, discovering medieval castles, exquisite palaces and churches that have been built in the baroque style.

Perhaps one of the most important reasons why you should consider visiting Bavaria is the Neuschwanstein Castle (http://www.neuschwanstein.de/; +4908362930830; Neuschwansteinstr. 20, 87645, Schwangau). Built by Ludwig II, this is a magnificent building to see, with a unique location. Visiting Bavaria, you will also have the opportunity to discover Wieskirche Pilgrimage Church (http://www.wieskirche.de/; +4908862932930; Wies 12, 86989, Steingaden) and the Roman Limes, which are splendid ancient fortifications.

Bavaria is famous for three tourist routes: the Romantic Road, the Castles Route and the German Alpine Road. Each tourist route will take you through different parts of Bavaria, allowing you to discover nature, architectural monuments and medieval palaces. For example, the Romantic Road extends over 400 km, going through Augsburg, Bad Mergentheim, Dinkelsbühl, Füssen, Harburg and Paffenwinkel. Regardless of the route you decide to take, Bavaria will remain in your mind forever, as the true taste of German living and you will certainly want to return to it.

Bavaria Local Travel Advice

Bavaria, Allgäu - Photo credit: pixabay.com

Bavaria is the perfect place to travel to, with so many tourist routes available, allowing you to discover both the beautiful nature and the cultural highlights. During your trip, I highly recommend that you try out our Bavarian cuisine, which is filled with mouth-watering delicacies. You have to try out the roasted pork, the authentic mountain cheese, the savory Bavarian doughnuts, the sweet mustard and our favorite snack, the salty pretzel. In terms of beverages, it is clear that Bavaria is the land of beer, so do not hesitate to try out one of the 40 types of beers (there are over 4000 brands of beer just in Bavaria). I can also personally recommended the wines from the Fraconia region and the traditional mountain schnapps, which is made from fruits (berries, peach and apples in particular).

In terms of weather, the finest month to see Bavaria is July, as this is the warmest month of the year (do not expect overbearing heat waves, however). In general, you can visit Bavaria between July and September. In fact, each season will allow you to see Bavaria from a completely different perspective. In winter, you will fall in love with the snow-capped mountains, enjoying the multitude of winter sports. In the spring, nature will be in full bloom, which is perfect for outdoor activities and recreation opportunities. In the fall, you can discover the most charming spectacle of nature, with the leaves colored in the most splendid colors. Any time you decide to come to Bavaria, you will be able to discover the countryside, which is peaceful and quiet, providing you with the necessary break from the bustling cities.

As I mentioned earlier, English is spoken and understood, but we appreciate when tourists make an effort to learn a couple of phrases. The Bavarian dialect is specific for this region and you will see that there are differences in the language spoken by those who live in the northern, central and southern part of Bavaria. A few useful words in Bavarian include: Sapperlot (used for expressing surprise but also for swearing), Servus (greeting, similar to hi/goodbye) and Seidla (beer mug of half a liter). Learning Bavarian phrases might help you have a more enjoyable experience as a tourist.

Bavaria on a Budget

Regensburg, Bavaria - Photo credit: pixabay.com

Traveling to Bavaria on a budget is possible, especially if you make the right choices. Perhaps the most important amount of money that you have to spend is on the transportation between the different areas of Bavaria, as well as the entry tickets to different museums or cultural attractions. If you want to save money, it is recommended that you purchase the Bayern Ticket, as this will provide you with the opportunity to travel in the Bavaria region for one day, with as many regional trains as you want. The one thing that you have to remember is that this ticket is valid only for the regional trains, in the 2nd class.

The Bayern Ticket also offers free access to the public transportation system in the different cities of Bavaria and also access to the regional bus services. Families can travel with their children, using this ticket (unlimited number of children, under the age of 15). Interestingly enough, this ticket will allow you to travel to regions outside Bavaria, such as: Ulm, Reutte, Kufstein and Salzburg.

The ticket is valid for 18 hours during the week and for 27 hours during the weekend. Its price is of €23 for one traveler, to which €5 are added for each additional traveler (up to five). The Bayern Ticket Night is available for those who want to travel only by night, costing €23 and an additional €2 for other travelers.

The Bayern Ticket can be purchased from the ticket machines that are commonly found in the train, S-Bahn or U-Bahn stations; keep in mind that, if you purchase the ticket from the counter, you will have to pay an additional €2.

If you are traveling to the Allgäu and Tirol region, or the Ammergauer Alpen, you should know that you can receive the Königs Card from your hotel. There is a special program, in which the hotels and B&Bs in the area take part, providing their guests with this card. It will give you free access to swimming pools, mountain railways and many more other things. As for the Black Forest region, you can either use the Konus Card (free transportation in the area) or the Schwarzwald Card (€32 for one person, provided discount to major tourist attractions in the area).

Bavaria Travel Basics

Bavaria Castle - Photo credit: pixabay.com

The most important thing that you have to remember is related to your passport. it should not expire within half a year of your travel, or you might have problems with the German authorities. In case you are traveling from outside Europe, you might need to use special plug adaptors for the electrical devices. Checking the weather can be helpful in determining which kind of clothing to pack but, when it comes to Bavaria, you should always be prepared for sudden changes in the weather and rain. The umbrella is not that useful as the raincoat, as the rain often comes with powerful winds. Apart from the rain coat, you should consider packing a pair of comfortable shoes, as you will do a lot of walking. Special shoes are recommended for trekking and, if you are coming during the winter, be sure to pack warm clothing and adequate equipment for winter sports. You should also be prepared for the weather phenomenon that is known as föhn, which is actually a warm and dry wind that comes from Italy. The reason why you need to be prepared, as this phenomenon can caused headaches and even mood swings in those who are sensitive to weather changes.

In regard to money, it is for the best that you carry some cash with you, as there may be restaurants and shops in which credit cards are not accepted. Also, you pay want to pay attention to the little things. For example, if you are using an escalator, keep in mind that the left side is for those who want to pass. The same goes for the bicycle lanes – walking on them, you risk getting hurt, as the majority of the bicyclists come at high speeds. Keep in mind that, throughout Bavaria, the stores are closed on Sundays and also on holidays. You may find gas stations open but nothing else, so do your shopping one day ahead.

The value added tax in Bavaria (and Germany in general) is of 19% and, if you keep the receipts for the products you have purchased, you can have this tax refunded at the airport. In case of large purchases, you might not be charged for this tax, so keep that in mind as well. As for the public restrooms, you should know that these can be used only after paying a small tax, generally varying between 30 and 50 cents.

Transportation in Bavaria

Bissenhofen, Bavaria - Photo credit: pixabay.com

If you are planning on traveling to different parts of Bavaria, you can make avail of the excellent public transportation system. Whether we are talking about the bus or the train service, it should be said that both means of transportation are safe and reliable. Plus, they are always on time, so you do not have to worry about waiting forever for your train/bus to come. It is true that some rural areas might be better reached with a personal car but, in general, both the bus and the train can represent good options for traveling around Bavaria.

Traveling with the public transportation is often faster than using a rental car and, as you will have the opportunity to see for yourself, you will enjoy how clean and safe the methods of transportation actually are. In terms of money, choosing the public transportation is a cheaper alternative to driving a car, especially if you want to travel between the large cities of Bavaria. If you want to plan your trip to perfection, you can use the Bayern-Fahrplan (http://www.bayern-fahrplan.de/auskunft-en/tripplanner), which is an electronic trip planning system recommended for those who want to travel throughout Bavaria by bus/train. This is also valid as an application that can be used on mobile devices, providing you with information on the schedules of the trains/buses, the chosen trajectory and ticket prices.

Traveling to Bavaria by train is certainly recommended, as you will have the opportunity to see the beautiful nature and create amazing memories. Keep in mind that the train system in Bavaria is highly efficient, having over 6200 km of railway and over 1000 train stations in which you can stop. Apart from that, there are really good connections that can be used in order to reach the rural areas. As it was already mentioned, you can purchase the Bayern Ticket and travel all over Bavaria, using just one ticket. This is the best way to travel indeed, exploring and discovering Bavaria by train!

Best Hotels and Restaurants in Bavaria

Oberammergau, Bavaria - Photo credit: pixabay.com

Bavaria is, without doubt, home to the finest hotels and restaurants in all Germany. In terms of hotels, you have the opportunity to find accommodation with splendid views, in rooms that are decorated with antique furnishings. The restaurants of Bavaria are renowned for their local specialties but also for the delicious food belonging to the international cuisine.

These are some of the best hotels in Bavaria:

1. The Rübezahl Hotel

- First class spa & romantic hotel

- Beautiful location – Bavarian Alps

- Picturesque and romantic landscape

- Panoramic view – Neuschwanstein & Hohenschwangau Castles
- Charming rooms and luxury suites
- Restaurant with local and international dishes
- Relaxation in the spa area
- Friendly atmosphere
- Address: Am Ehberg 31, Schwangau, 87645
- Tel.: +49083628888

Website: http://www.hotelruebezahl.de/

2. The Schloss Elmau Retreat

- Spectacular view – Wetterstein Mountain, Ferchenbach Creek
- 47 suites, 3 restaurants and lounge with library and terrace
- Yoga pavilion and spa
- High level of hospitality
- Elegant interior decorations
- Swimming pool
- Address: 82493 Elmau
- Tel.: +4908823180
- Website: http://www.schloss-elmau.de/en/

3. Ulrichshof Baby & Kinder Bio-Resort

First European bio-children hotel

Splendid location – Bavarian Forest

Only families with children

Children under the age of 6 – free stay

Best place for a family holiday

Meals prepared from 100% organic food

Address: Zettisch 42, 93485 Rimbach

Tel.: +49099779500

Website: http://www.ulrichshof.com/en/

These are some of the best restaurants in Bavaria:

1. Restaurant Überfahrt

- Exquisite dining experience

- Beautiful interior décor

- Opportunity to taste local dishes from the alpine region

- Amazing blend between rustic and sophisticated tastes

- Also has dishes from international cuisine

- Address: Überfahrtstrasse 10, Rottach-Egern, 83700

- Tel.: +4908022/669-0

- Website: http://www.seehotel-ueberfahrt.com/

2. Gourmetrestaurant Reiterzimmer

- Culinary delights in an elegant atmosphere

- Bavarian delicacies, with produce from the local region

- Exclusive wine menu includes over 900 wines (European wines)

- Address: Ramsachstrasse 8, Murnau am Staffelsee, 82418

- Tel.: +4908841/491-0

- Website: http://www.alpenhof-murnau.com/

3. Acquarello

- Meals that are created through artistic inspiration

- Italian cuisine, dishes of amazing taste

- Recommended choices – vitello tonnato, fried zucchini flowers and ravioli fille with ricotta and walnut

- Excellent wine selection

- Amazing desserts (especially the mint ice cream)
- Address: Mühlbaurstrasse 36, München, Bogenhausen, 81677
- Tel.: +49089/4704848
- Website: http://www.acquarello/de/

Bavaria Cultural Highlights

Bavaria Village Festival - Photo credit: pixabay.com

Bavaria's cultural calendar is filled throughout the entire year, providing tourists with a number of opportunities to discover this part of Germany at its finest. Between June 19th and August 2nd, there is the European Weeks Festival (http://www.ew-passau.de), organized in Pass

au. Each year, a different motto is chosen for this festival, with the one for 2015 being: "meet worlds, discover people". From June 21st to July 31st, there is the famous Munich Opera Festival (http://www.bayerische-staatsoper.de), bringing international artists on the stage of the Bavarian State Opera.

If you are all about summer festivals, then you definitely have to check out the Fraconian Summer Festival (http://www.fraenkischer-sommer.de), taking place between June and August. Between July 25th and August 28th, you can attend the Richard Wagner Festspiele Bayreuth (http://www.bayreuther-festspiele.de); this is one of the most important festivals in Bavaria, presenting the music dramas of the famous Richard Wagner. Another important event of Bavaria is the MusikHochGenuss (http://www.allgaeu-festivals.de), taking place in Allgäu, between March and October. During this period, there are a number of concerts organized nearby Bavaria's famous castles and palaces; the cultural program represents the perfect opportunity for a musical journey, delighting you with choices that range from classical music to jazz.

The Kaltenberg Medieval Tournament (http://www.ritterturnier.de/en/) is definitely worth visiting, being organized in Kaltenberg, each July. If you want to go back to the medieval times and see knights and jesters, listening to medieval music, this is the best place for you to be. Or perhaps you might be interested in the castle concerts that are organized at the famous Neuschwanstein Castle (http://www.schwangau.de/), taking place in September. The Coburg Samba Festival (http://www.samba-festival.de) is also worth your time, being the largest samba festival that takes place outside of Brazil. Taking place between July 10th and 12th, it has an amazing parade, a samba party that starts early in the morning and music that is a complete delight.

In conclusion, Bavaria has splendid choices when it comes to cultural events and you can organize a tour of Bavaria just by going from one event to the other. As you have seen for yourself, the majority of the events are organized in the summer or at the start of autumn, at the weather is at its finest.

Shopping In Bavaria

Bavaria Postcards - Photo credit: pixabay.com

Given the unique culture of Bavaria, you can expect that your shopping experience is unique as well. You cannot come to this part of Germany and not purchase the traditional folklore costumes, the Dirndl for the ladies and the lederhosen for the gentlemen. These are an essential part of the Bavarian culture and they can remind you of the times you spent here. Traditional Bavarian souvenirs can be found in small shops, as well as handicrafts. Perhaps you will decide to purchase a beer mug as a keepsake, or several fridge magnets to give to your friends.

Each town in Bavaria has elegant and intimate small boutiques that are nestled in the historic center. Here, you can find products that belong to the traditional Bavarian culture, as well as items of clothing or footwear belonging to international brands. If you want to taste the local food, it is recommended that you visit the farmer's markets that are organized in each town on a regular basis. You can also visit the rummage fairs, as you can find a lot of souvenirs here at great prices. As for the holidays, the best time to visit Bavaria is around Christmas, when you can find amazing shopping opportunities at the different Christmas markets.

If you are interested in outlet shopping opportunities, one of the most recommended choices is the Ingoldstadt Village (http://www.ingoldstadtvillage.com/). This is located in Ingoldstadt and it offers some pretty amazing choices for shopping, including products that belong to internationally-renowned brands. Ingoldstadt Village is located at a close distance from Munich and it offers items of clothing, footwear, beauty, home and décor. On the plus side, it has an area filled with restaurants and coffee shops, destined for relaxation after a day of shopping.

Why Come to Salzburg?

Salzburg Aerial View - Photo credit: pixabay.com

Salzburg is one of the biggest cities in Austria, being visited by over 5.5 million of people each year. One of the most important reasons that should bring you to Salzburg is the amazing baroque architecture. Walking around in Salzburg, it is practically impossible not to notice the wonderful buildings and also how well they have been preserved. In fact, Salzburg has been added to the UNESCO World Heritage Sites in 1997, being one of the cities with the best preserved historic centers north of Alps.

As a tourist, you need to come and discover the charm of Salzburg, with its elegant palaces, amazing museums and beautiful historic center. You need to walk on the cobbled streets, to drink a glass of chilled wine and take it all in. Salzburg will charm you with its relaxed atmosphere but you should also consider traveling to the surrounding areas of the town, discovering the scenic alpine surroundings. The best thing about Salzburg is that it can be visited in both the winter and the summer, allowing you to enjoy different activities. The surrounding areas of Salzburg provide opportunities for winter sports but also for summer activities, such as hiking or bicycling.

The town of Salzburg entices you with food that belongs to both national and international cuisine. In fact, Salzburg has been named one of the fine food European capitals. Tourists who come here have the chance to taste regional delicacies, generally prepared from produce that have been grown locally. Many restaurants provide niche products that come from organic farmers, such as different types of cheeses. Salzburg is and will remain a paradise for wine lovers, with an excellent selection of wines being offered at elegant wine bars.

If you are still looking for reasons to come to Salzburg, consider its main attractions: Salzburg Cathedral (http://www.salzburger-dom.at/; +4366280477950; Domplatz 1a), Hohensalzburg Castle (http://www.salzburg-burgen.at/de/hohensalzburg/; +4366284243011; Mönchsberg 34), Franciscan Church (http://www.franziskaner.at; +43662843629; Franziskanergasse 5), St Peter's Abbey (http://www.stift-stpeter.at/; +43662844576; Sankt-Peter-Bezirk 1), Salzburg Residenz (http://www.salzburg-burgen.at/de/residenz/; +4366280422690; Residenzpl. 1), Mozart's Birthplace (http://www.mozartmuseum.at/; +43662844313; Getreidegasse 9), Mozart's Residence (http://www.mozartmuseum.at/; +4366287422740; Makartpl. 8), Mirabell Palace (http://www.salzburg/info; +4366280720; Mirabellplatz 4), and Hellbrunn (http://www.hellbrunn.at/; +436628203720; Fürstenweg 37).

Salzburg Local Travel Advice

Mirabell Park - Photo credit: pixabay.com

As it was already mentioned, Salzburg once was the city in which the famous movie "The Sound of Music" was filmed. I highly recommend visiting the gardens of the beautiful Mirabell Palace, as this is where Julie Andrews and the von Trapps once sang and danced. It will be like a journey back in time and you will definitely get goosebumps walking around the same rose beds and fountains. If you are looking for a unique experience, consider going to Gaisberg, which is a nearby mountain peak. You can take the bus from Mirabellaplatz in order to reach the top of Gaisberg, enjoying the view of Salzburg and also of the surrounding lakes from up there.

Salzburg is, without doubt, the city of Mozart. This is the reason why you have to go and check out the birthplace of Mozart. You can see the modest chambers in which he lived for a brief period of time and admire the tiny violin on which he played as a toddler. In Salzburg, you can also visit the house in which he lived afterwards, which is just as modest and yet beautiful as his birth house. As you will see, the shops are filled with Mozart souvenirs, whether we are talking about the famous chocolates with marzipan filling or other small keepsakes.

In case you decide to visit Schloss Hellbrunn, I have to advise you about the trick fountains. These were designed to squirt water at guests and they still serve their purpose today. Do not sit on the stone chairs, trying to imagine how it was like back in the old days, as water will come out and you will have an unpleasant surprise. If you want to enjoy a traditional pint of beer, be sure to visit the Augustiner Brästübl (http://www.augustinerbiert.at/; +4366243124620), one of the largest taverns in Austria. The Afro Café (http://www.afrocafe.at; +43662844888; Bürgerspitalpl. 5) can provide you with the most delicious Ethiopian coffee but you should also consider tasting the African tea. Also, during your stay in Salzburg, do not hesitate to try out the famous Austrian schnitzel (made from fried veal, with a coat of egg and breadcrumbs) and the mouth-watering apple strudel.

Salzburg On A Budget

Salzach River (Night) - Photo credit: pixabay.com

Salzburg is somewhat of a live museum, with its amazing architecture and the beautiful river Salzach. Walking around Salzburg does not cost anything and you have the opportunity to discover one of the most beautiful cities in the world. The strong point of Salzburg is the historic center, with its old buildings that are amazingly well kept. You can take a romantic stroll on the banks of Salzach or visit the beautiful Steingasse, located on the right bank of the river. The cobbled streets and the buildings that are practically covered in ivy will bring out the romantic in you. If you are interested in discovering the natural beauty of Salzburg, it is recommended that you visit the Mirabell gardens (free of charge as well). Or, if you are up for a little bit more effort, you can go on a hiking trip up to Mönchsberg Hill. For those who are interested in reaching the hill, without putting in no effort, there is a lift that can be taken (it costs only €2).

The majority of the tourist attractions in Salzburg provide discounts for students and seniors, upon presenting a legitimation card. However, as a regular tourist, you can save a lot of money by purchasing the Salzburg Card. This is a tourist card that grants free admission to numerous tourist attractions, including the Fortress Funicular, the Untersberg Cableway and the Salzach ship service. Apart from that, during the validity of the card, you can benefit from free public transportation and enjoy the discounts offered for concerts and theater performances.

The Salzburg Card is offered with a free brochure, in which you will find all the information on the tourist attractions that you can visit with this card. It is valid for 24, 48 or 72 hours, with prices varying according to the period of validity. Between January-April and November-December, these are the prices of the Salzburg Card: 24 hours - €24 (adult), €12 (children 6-15 years); 48 hours - €32 (A), €16 (C); 72 hours - €37 (A), €18.50 (C). Between May-October, the prices are: 24 hours - €27 (adult), €13.50 (children 6-15 years); 48 hours - €36 (A), €18 (C); 72 hours - €42 (A), €21 (C). With this card, you can also take a bus tour of the city (with audio guide included) and you won't have to stand in line for a ticket to different attractions.

Salzburg Travel Basics

Mozart Geburtshaus - Photo credit: pixabay.com

In case you are wondering when it's the best time to visit Salzburg, you should know that this is a perfect choice, no matter the season or the time of year. However, you can plan your travel according to the different events that take place here; for example, you can come in July or August, taking part in the Salzburger Festspiele, listening to amazing performances of classical music and opera. Or, if you want to discover even more about Mozart, you can visit Salzburg in January, being part of the famous Mozartwoche (Week of Mozart). December is also a good month to visit Salzburg, especially around Christmas. The traditional Christmas markets open, with their delicious Glühwein (warm wine with rum and spices) and there are plenty of opportunities for winter sports around Salzburg.

You can arrive to Salzburg by plane, landing on Salzburg Airport. Both national and international flights land here and you can take the bus from the airport, traveling to the main train station (which is located in the city center as well). If you are coming from countries outside the European Union, you will need a valid passport in order to enter Austria and you cannot remain here for more than 90 days (after that, you will require a visa). Citizens who are part of the European Union can come to Salzburg, using only their ID card.

Even though English is well understood in Salzburg, it might be useful to learn a few phrases in Austrian German, such as: "Hallo" (hello), "Tschüss" (informal goodbye), "Danke" (thank you), "Bitte" (welcome), "Prost" (Cheers). These words are going to help you approach the friendly people in Salzburg, especially in restaurants or bars. Also, keep in mind that if you are traveling to Salzburg in the fall, it can get quite chilly and you might need some warm clothing for the night. You will see that, despite being chilly, everyone prefers to stay outside, wrapped comfortably in a blanket and nursing a good bottle of wine.

In terms of transportation, if you decide to travel by car, do not forget to purchase the vignette for the road, as soon as you have entered Austria. The price is of €7 for 10 days and do not hesitate to apply the sticker on the window. The police checks cars frequently for the vignette and it would be a shame to get a fine. Other from that, keep in mind that the historic center is a pedestrianized area and that the best way to see everything is by walking. Keep your car at your hotel garage, as the parking around Salzburg can be quite hectic and expensive.

Transportation Options In Salzburg

Salzburg Funicular - Photo credit: pixabay.com

The public transportation system in Salzburg is well-developed and it can save you the effort of finding a parking space. No matter which hotel you decide to use for accommodation or how far it may be from the Altstadt (old part of town), keep in mind that all routes go to the city center. Among the choices you have available for transportation, there are: environmentally-friendly trolley bus, regular bus, S-Bahn (city train). Both the trolley buses and the regular buses come at 10 minute-intervals, so you do not have to worry about waiting forever.

In regard to the tickets, the same ticket is valid for all means of transportation. So, you do not have to purchase a different ticket if you want to use the trolley bus, then switch to other methods of transportation. The tickets can be purchased from small kiosks or from the machines that are found at the bus stops; if you forget to buy the ticket, you can buy one from the driver at a more expensive price. As soon as you got on the bus, do not forget to validate your ticket. Otherwise, you can get a fine.

The tickets are available for a set period of time; however, if you decide to spend more time in Salzburg, you can purchase a 24-hour ticket or a weekly pass. Keep in mind that children aged between 6 and 14 years travel with the public transportation at a discounted price. Also, if you decide to purchase the Salzburg Card, you have free transportation for the period the card is valid.

For the night transportation, you have specific means of transportation available, such as the bus taxi or the night express. And if you want to reach the fortress up on the hill, you can use the cable railway, which is included in the public transportation system as well. Renting a bike is also a good idea, as the cycling paths are well developed in Salzburg; on the plus side, there is no better choice of transportation during rush hours other than a bike.

Best Hotel And Restaurants In Salzburg

Hotel Bristol - Photo credit: pixabay.com

Salzburg is home to a number of fine hotels and restaurants, many of them having a long tradition. The most beautiful hotels overlook the Salzach River or the splendid fortress on the hill, reminding of the old Austrian imperial charm. The restaurants of Salzburg provide dishes that belong to both local and international cuisine, being appreciated for their beautiful interior decorations as well.

These are some of the finest hotels in Salzburg:

1. Hotel Goldener Hirsch

- Located on the famous Getreidegasse

- Beautiful blend between tradition and modern
- Luxury hotel, located in a historical building
- Cordial warmth and hospitality
- Excellent restaurant
- Unique interior décor (Austrian style)
- State-of-the-art amenities
- Address: Getreidegasse 37
- Tel.: +4366280840
- Website: http://www.goldenerhirsch.com/

2. Hotel Sacher

- Great location, right in the heart of the city
- Splendid view over the Salzach River and the Hohensalzburg fortress
- 113 rooms and suites
- Historic elegance
- All rooms equipped with modern amenities and antique furnishings
- Amazing restaurant and café (best place to taste the original Sacher Torte)
- Address: Schwarzstrasse 5-7
- Tel: +43662889770
- Website: http://www.sacher.com/

3. Hotel Bristol

- Grand hotel
- Located vis-à-vis from the Old Town
- Stay in the same hotel as Sigmund Freud
- Lavish decorated rooms
- Front rooms have the best views
- Address: Makartplatz 4

- Tel.: +436628735576
- Website: http://www.bristol-salzburg.at/

These are some of the finest restaurants in Salzburg:

2. Magazin

- Great restaurant to taste local dishes
- Located west of the Old Town
- Recommended choice – octopus dish
- Modern décor
- Excellent selection of wines
- Address: Augustinergasse 13
- Tel.: +436628415840
- Website: http://www.magazin.co.at/

2. M32

- Unique location – hilltop (you can also find a very nice art gallery near it)
- Wonderful decors, with bold colors
- Terrace tables provide splendid views over the hilltop fortress
- The dishes are delicious and light
- Recommended choice – tomato soup with dumplings
- Address: Mönchsberg 32
- Tel.: +43662841000
- Website: http://www.m32.at/

3. Stifskeller St Peter

- Dine in the same restaurant as Charlemagne and Mozart
- One of the oldest restaurants in Salzburg

- Recommended choices – traditional Austrian schnitzel, goose liver parfait and calvados sorbet

- Address: St Peter Bezkirk 1-4

- Tel.: +43662841268

- Website: http://www.haslauer.at/

Cultural Highlights In Salzburg

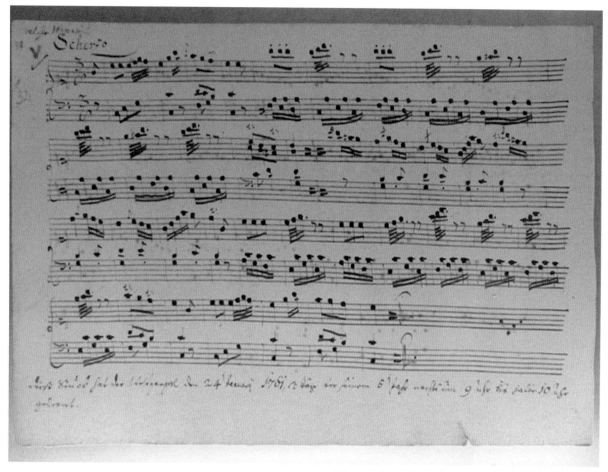

Mozart Music - Photo credit: pixabay.com

Salzburg is a city of culture, with over 4000 cultural events taking place each year. Cultural geniuses such as Mozart, Haydn and Zweig have left their influence on Salzburg and their presence is felt even today. Among the most interesting cultural events that you can attend in Salzburg, there are: Mozart Week (January), Whitsuntide Festival, Salzburg Festival (summertime), Jazzherbst (concerts) and Advent concerts (around Christmas).

The Salzburg Festival takes place between July and August, bringing in millions of tourists to Salzburg. There are over 180 cultural events organized during the festival, including operas, concerts, theatre and readings. The interesting thing is that the theme changes from year to year. Mozart Week is a music festival that is organized annually, in order to celebrate the birthday of Mozart. The festival takes place each year in January.

The Whitsuntide Festival is a music festival that is organized on an annual basis as well, during which there are a wide range of cultural events. You can see amazing opera performances and listen to choral and orchestral concerts. In autumn, there is the Jazzherbst Festival, a music festival dedicated to the jazz style of music. Organized in late autumn, apart from jazz concerts, it also includes films and exhibitions. Around Christmas, there is nothing better than attending one of the lovely Advent concerts.

There are many more other cultural events that you can discover during your stay in Salzburg, including the Salzburg Biennale, the Salzburg Culture Days and the contemporary Dialoge Festival. In Salzburg, there is always something to see and discover, with the majority of the cultural events being organized in stylish settings.

The Shopping Opportunities of Salzburg

Getreidegasse - Photo credit: pixabay.com

Salzburg is a shopping paradise for all tourists who arrive in this town, providing a unique experience. Some of the most amazing shops can be found in the historic center, especially on the Getreidegasse and Judengasse. Plus, there are many traditional passageways, in which there are lovely boutiques filled with all sort of products. The shops of Salzburg have a long traditional, especially the small boutiques but, today, one can also find shops in which international, luxury brands are present.

Those who have a taste for tradition should visit the traditional shops of Austrian manufacturers near the Getreidegasse. There are delicious bakeries to be discovered, along with the finest liquors and custom-made suits. Some of the shops have become tourist attractions on their own, such as the pharmacy in the historic center, the Holzermayr chocolate shops or St Peter's bakery. Other shops that are great for shopping and visiting include the Anton Koppenwallner goldsmith shop and the Schatz confectionery. Also, do not forget to visit the traditional souvenir shops, purchasing small trinkets for your loved ones.

Apart from the shops in the Old City, one can also enjoy one of the most amazing shopping centers in the entire world. Europark (http://www.europark.at) has an impressive number of 130 stores and you can make an entire day out of shopping here, the choices being both modern and attractive. The shops are open from 10 to 18 from Monday to Friday and between 10 and 17 on Saturday. Some shops might have a lunch break and the majority of the shops are closed on Sundays and holidays. However, you may be able to find some shops open on Sundays, including those that sell souvenirs.

Conclusion

Bavaria is considered one of the most beautiful parts of Germany and for all the right reasons. The main star of Bavaria is Munich, a city that is as elegant and it is modern. And, if you happen to come to Bavaria and Munich, it would be a shame not to visit Salzburg as well. In Munich, you will find yourself drawn to the numerous, traditional beer halls, not to mention the varied museums and amazing buildings that have been reconstructed after the war. Bavaria will amaze you with its one-of-a-kind castles, including the famous Newschwanstein Castle, which was built by King Ludwig and the breathtaking alpine scenery.

In Bavaria, you can enjoy the beauty of nature, hiking on green mountain hills during the summer and skiing on the same slopes during the winter. You can explore the ruins of medieval castles, visit villages and taste the delicious local cuisine. As an explorer that you have become, you can take one of the tourist routes that exist in Bavaria, following on the steps of the famous Sisi Empress. From there, Salzburg is just one step away. The city of Mozart will dazzle you with its splendid architecture, amazing cultural agenda and unique architecture. In Salzburg, you can go on a boat ride on the Salzach River and prepare yourself to be amazed. The boat

Made in the USA
Middletown, DE
22 April 2020